Insurance Laid Bare

The Naked Facts About an Unsexy Topic

By

Marc Schwartz

This book is dedicated to:

My lovely and faithful wife, Gloria, who indulges me in all the personal and business ventures I have managed to stumble into, but always reminds me of the realities.

Table of Contents

Introduction

Congratulations. You obviously have an intrepid nature to want to learn more about insurance. We will be covering not only personal insurance of various types, but business insurance. So, the book should appeal to a broad spectrum of curious people.

Why am I writing a book about insurance?

Because I can, and I have the experience. More than 35 years of experience. As they say, teachers must teach, and I am a teacher. This book is a compilation of new articles and ones I have already published. It is anything but exhaustive, but hopefully it is interesting and informative all the way from how to read an insurance policy to many of the different types of insurance and how they work. I try to answer why restaurant insurance is different from auto repair garage insurance.

The most difficult question for me has been "to whom do I want to direct this book?" Insurance agents? Possibly. There are parts of this book that will be of interest to agents who want to move into commercial insurance (my specialty.) but I can't make this a textbook, because nobody else will want to read it—too complex.

Business individuals might be interested. Restaurant owners might be particularly interested in their section, as would owners of other businesses that are mentioned. Individuals who hate insurance might be interested if they hate it because they don't understand it. There are parts of this book that will help.

Again, I am not writing a textbook. I want people reading it to stay awake, not be lulled to sleep. This is more an overview that will get you through the process and help identify some of the pitfalls. Maybe you will even look at insurance with more kindness by understanding what it is trying to do.

All the examples of claims and loss come from my own experience as an agent. In thirty plus years, there has been plenty of time to amass examples. I only hope they are interesting and informative. With a topic so potentially technical that is a fine line to walk.

Now, let's get started. I will begin by defining insurance, then go into the different forms of coverage, and then provide examples of common and less common forms of coverage.

PART I: Insurance Basics

Chapter One: What Is Insurance

How Does It Work?

Suppose you and nine other people buy a boat. You want to protect that boat in the event that it burns, sinks, or suffers some other catastrophe. The boat is valued at, say, $100,000. That means each of you is at risk for $10,000 in case of loss.

So, you all decide to pool your resources and tuck away $10,000 each in case of a loss. This is called spreading the risk. And insurance companies refer to the owners of an insurance policy as "the risk." Don't be offended; it is purely a subjective reference.

Suppose instead that there are ten boats to insure, each with ten owners and each boat is worth $100,000. That is a total value for the "risks" of $1,000,000, and the risk is spread among 100 owners. Each owner now still has $10,000 of risk.

But now, the collective owners begin to look at the different boats. Some have leaky gas tanks. Some are not maintained very well, or are docked next to a fueling station, or are left with the keys in the boat and otherwise unlocked. The responsible owners might think that the irresponsible owners should possibly pay more than $10,000 and the more responsible owners should pay less, since they are creating less risky conditions. This is now called underwriting; determining the amount of risk and charging accordingly.

The number of risk factors is many, and the underwriters have a big job, but ultimately this is how the premiums are decided. Also, if for example the loss rate is one boat in ten for every year, you might be able to break the premium up into $1000 per year on average for each owner (more for each irresponsible owner and conversely, less for more responsible owners.) Age, condition, location, amount of use and many other factors come into play, but this is how the first underwriters created insurance.

Who Are the Parties to an Insurance Policy?

The insured is considered the first party. The insurance company is considered the second party, and everybody not associated with the first two is considered a third party.

Property coverage: this protects the property of the first party. It could be a boat, a home, a car or a business, but it is meant to make whole the owner of the property and the insurance contract.

Liability coverage is meant to protect the owner of the property from third party lawsuits. If you run over a skier on your boat, he would certainly sue you, and your liability coverage is designed to protect you.

The exact details of how you are covered for property and liability by perils of environment and action are defined by the policy you purchase. And that is where the fine print comes in. It is important to know the facts of the fine print.

One more thing; the policy starts at the exact minute and date when a policy is bound. I have had a walk-in customer want to write an auto policy immediately. I came to find out later that that he had had a traffic accident that morning, did not have current auto insurance and thought that if he wrote a policy that day, it would retroactively cover his accident. Had we not had an exact date and time of insurance binding, he might have gotten away with it.

They Don't Insure a Sure Thing

That brings up another subject. Insurance companies will not insure you if you are aware of impending losses. I had a young woman call me to say she wanted that renter's policy I had quoted for her some time ago—the one she did not buy. Problem is that "the fires were a couple of blocks away" and she wanted to cover herself for that impending loss. Nope. It does not work that way.

Insurance agents are eager to write a policy on just about anyone who appears in the doorway. I recall one small clothing store that wanted coverage. The owners were a bit cagey about information of ownership and property coverage. Too suspicious. They must have procured insurance somewhere, and later I noticed that half of the shopping center had burned down, destroying the business of one of my clients in that same center. Arson was suspected. I decline to write coverage on such cagey situations.

And by the way, don't think of misrepresenting material facts on an application. If you do, the insurance company has the right to revoke the coverage as if you were never covered. They might happily refund all of the premium you paid and deny the claim. Or they might mitigate the payout if the situation warrants it.

Chapter Summary/Key Takeaways

Insurance is similar to a loan. Put yourself in the position of a lender. Ask yourself what you would like to know about the person or business to whom you will be lending $1,000,000. Would you like to know how reliable they are? Do they have the ability to pay premiums? Are they representing the risk honestly? What are they hiding that could lead to a claim?

Accidents happen. That's why we have insurance. But Insurance Companies don't want to insure a loss that is sure to happen.

Let's learn about some personal insurance next. We will begin with personal automobile coverage in the next chapter. We will cover the most common personal types of insurance, and then move into commercial insurance.

Part II: Personal Insurance

Chapter Two: Individual Auto Insurance

The Basics

Ah, yes. Personal auto insurance.

This is probably the first thing most people think of when you mention insurance. It is required in order to be able to drive a vehicle on public roads.

The coverages for auto insurance include both property and liability. Property insurance takes the form of comprehensive and collision. Comprehensive covers damage to the vehicle (broadly speaking) when it is not moving, and collision (seems obvious) covers physical damage to the vehicle when it is moving (mostly.) Think of broken or damaged windshields or side windows, or theft of a radio from the vehicle as comprehensive coverage.

The collision coverage is on an "actual cash value" basis (new term,) which means that it covers what the vehicle is worth at the time of the accident. If the cost of repair is higher than the value of the vehicle, it will not get repaired. You will just get a check instead for the value of the vehicle. And by the way, you may not like the amount of the check. Some companies are more generous than others.

There are exceptions—gap coverage can cover the gap between the value of the vehicle and the amount you still owe on the loan, but basically the vehicle value gets depreciated. If you have a classic vehicle that is worth more than its residual value by virtue of its art value, you would have to get an appraisal prior to the incident. If the vehicle gets stolen or totaled, the appraised value will prevail. There are special insurance companies for classic vehicles, as this is where most of these situations reside.

There will be deductibles on both comprehensive and collision coverage, which can vary the premium that you pay. Also, and very importantly, this coverage is not required. If you want to self-insure the value of the vehicle (let's say it is a very old one with little remaining value,) you may choose not to cover that portion of the auto insurance.

Liability coverage is not optional in most states. The coverage is available from very low to pretty high. In California you can get $15,000 all the way up to $500,000. The consideration is what you can afford to lose if you hurt someone else. It covers both bodily injury and property damage (someone else's vehicle, or a lamppost or possibly a fire hydrant.)

A colleague of mine had a client who was driving on the freeway when a pedestrian ran across the freeway. The driver hit him, and his leg had to be amputated. Loss of a leg would not be covered by $15,000 and possibly not even by $500,000, but more coverage is always better. I'm speaking mainly about California, where there are many attorneys waiting in line to file suit.

Other Coverages and Pitfalls

There are other coverages on auto policies:

Uninsured motorist coverage protects the driver in case he is injured by another driver who is uninsured or underinsured. In "no-fault states" this is the main coverage. Each person's own coverage protects him and there is no liability coverage requirement.

Medical coverage for incidental medical payments without a lawsuit being filed.

Towing, car rental, deductible buyback and such are all bells and whistles that can be added to a policy.

When buying a policy, if you will be driving another vehicle not insured by you from time to time, it is important to make sure your policy's liability coverage goes with you, and goes at full limits, not minimum limits. And see if your vehicle is covered for someone else driving your car on occasion. Many insurance carriers quote more competitive rates by not covering these conditions. Buyer beware.

And while we are at it, let's talk about Uber and Lyft. Are you driving for either of them? that's what is called "livery service" in commercial parlance. Commercial premiums are very high for livery service because it is high risk. That undoubtedly means that your current insurance company won't cover you as an operator. Either get Uber or Lyft to cover you or make sure your current insurance policy will cover you. Otherwise, there could be a very large claim at some point, and you won't have protection.

Motorcycle insurance is structured similarly to auto insurance. I would not skimp on liability coverage, as a motorcycle is a serious hunk of metal at speed and can hurt someone. Similarly, I would not skimp on uninsured motorist coverage nor medical coverage. One is pretty vulnerable on a motorcycle.

Chapter Summary/Key Takeaways

There is a lot more to auto insurance than most people know when they buy. Have good questions to ask when buying. What exactly is specific to your particular situation? If you only go by price, you may have a rude surprise at some point.

So, take the time to find out what you are getting for your money.

In the next chapter we will cover the next most common personal insurance, dwellings.

Chapter Three: Dwellings and Homes

The Different Types

Dwelling policies are meant to protect dwellings of all sorts. They normally include property coverage and liability coverage, but the perils that they protect from are written differently. They have different designations.

HO-1 is called a basic form policy. it is a named peril coverage, and the perils it names and covers are: Fire or smoke, Explosions, Lightning, Hail and windstorms, Theft/malicious mischief, Vandalism, Damage from vehicles, Damage from aircraft, Riots and civil commotion, Volcanic eruption.

It does not include liability coverage nor coverage for personal items within the dwelling. Also, property is covered on an ACV or actual cash value basis. That is the depreciated value of the dwelling, not the replacement cost value.

HO-2 Broad form coverage. This form does cover liability and personal property plus some other items, and the list of perils is broader than the basic form policy, but it is still a named peril policy as opposed to an HO-3, which is comprehensive.

HO-3 Special form. This is the policy most often written for homeowners. It covers the dwelling on a special form basis with replacement cost (not market value.) There is no list of perils, only a small list of exclusions such as nuclear hazard, earthquake, flood, hurricane, mold and a few others. Personal property is covered on a named peril basis. Unattached structures are also covered. Loss of use is typically covered, which pays for living expenses after a covered loss when the owners have to move to temporary quarters.

Different insurance carriers may provide different additions to the original coverage protections, so it is important to review exactly what is covered and what is not. Decide what is important in your situation.

HO-4 renters policies protect a renter, who needs coverage only for his contents and for liability. It typically also covers loss of use.

HO-5 comprehensive all risk contents. This is an HO-3 policy with better coverage for contents. It is written on higher end homes and is more costly than HO-3, but of course it protects more fully. It is worth your while if you want to better protect your contents.

HO-6 condominium (or townhouse) coverage. Since the owner of a condo does not own the structure, this form covers interior structures (cabinets, flooring, fixtures) in addition to contents and liability and loss of use. It also has a loss assessment coverage, which would cover the assessment that the homeowner's association might levy if there were a loss of structure to a covered peril. The coverage for interior structures and loss of use are variable, and the policy owner should make sure there is sufficient coverage for each type of contingency.

HO-7 mobile home coverage. This type of policy is similar to an HO-3 policy, but is written for mobile homes, so may not cover separate structures.

Chapter Summary/Key Takeaways

As before, all of the above policies have variations depending on the insurance company that writes the coverage. As with Auto Insurance, it is critical to ask questions and compare to determine which is best for you.

We will cover Flood Insurance next.

Chapter Four: Flood Coverage

Not Your Usual Home Insurance.

Interestingly, property insurance coverage, both personal and commercial, does not cover rising water and earth movement. If you are in a heavy rainstorm and the damage comes not as a result of wind driven rain, but of rising water. Homeowners insurance will not cover it.

Neither will Homeowners insurance cover the muddy hill in back of your house sliding into your den by way of the glass patio door. Both of those situations are strictly the domain of flood insurance.

Flood insurance is created and underwritten by FEMA, the government agency. It may be sold and administered through third party companies.

The rating factors are:

1. Flood severity zones, which are assigned a rating number based on potential for flooding. Elevation and proximity to sources of water are influencers.
2. Susceptibility of your structure and contents to damage, based on which structure level they are located. First story—more expensive. Second story, less so.

Lenders may require such coverage if they are lending on a structure in a flood zone.

There is normally a thirty-day waiting period between application and issuance of the policy, just to make sure the flood is not imminent at the time the policy is purchased. Insurance companies hate to insure sure losses, and FEMA is no exception. They want you to buy when the chances are more random—go figure.

Let's cover additional liability next

Chapter Five: Umbrellas

More Liability Coverage When You Need It

The term, umbrella, is a metaphor for what the project covers.

An umbrella is a type of insurance coverage which adds extra liability coverage on top of the underlying coverage of a group of policies. It adds to liability limits. It is not property coverage.

Automobile coverage usually tops out at $500,000 of liability coverage, as does homeowner insurance. If you have lots of assets, you may want to protect yourself with higher limits. That would protect you in the event of a large lawsuit.

For personal insurance policies, it would enhance the limits of your autos, homes, rental properties, motorcycles, jet skis and other such possessions. It is overarching, and thus, it is called an umbrella. Many celebrities and other wealthy people have $10 million and $20 million or higher limits to protect them. How much value have you amassed by this time in your life? Maybe an umbrella is for you.

Underlying coverage of highest limits may be required, or slightly less than maximum limits may be required for more premium.

The form is a following form, so it covers whatever the underlying coverage is. There may be some coverage additional to the underlying coverage, in which case, it might have its own deductible, called a "drop down."

Commercial umbrellas are very similar to personal umbrellas, except that they go over commercial general liability, auto liability and workers compensation coverages. Some municipalities and very large companies require them if a vendor is going to do business with them, or a contractor is going to do work for them. They may require very high limits.

Excess liability policies are also available, sometimes from the same insurance carrier that provides the underlying policy. The difference is that the coverage only goes over the policy over which it is written, so it is not a true umbrella. It is also a following form, but due to its character is more limited.

> Let's discuss another important type of coverage next: Earthquake.

Chapter Six: Earthquake Insurance

Personal Earthquake Coverage

Personal lines earthquake coverage is designed to reimburse for damage to a structure and contents as a result of an earthquake. Availability and cost vary widely depending on location, due to proximity to earthquake faults. There are also different forms of earthquake coverage, which protect differently, and costs vary. Deductibles also vary, creating more differences in premium.

There are two main types of coverage. One type of coverage is called combined single limit. This has a single protection amount, and it lumps contents, loss of use and structure all into one coverage amount. The problem with this form of coverage is that there is a single, large deductible, based on the full amount of coverage provided. After an earthquake, if only contents are damaged and the deductible takes into account structure as well, the deductible could very well exceed the amount of contents and coverage would be nil. This type of coverage is less expensive than comprehensive earthquake coverage, as it is less likely to pay out.

Comprehensive coverage has a separate coverage for structure, for unattached structures (fences and garages,) and contents. Each portion has its own deductible, so it is more likely to pay out after an event. Naturally it is more expensive than a combined single limit policy.

Loss of use and loss assessment coverage both exist in both types of coverage, and amounts are governed by the limits provided. Fortunately, these last two can usually be varied such that anticipated loss of use and assessments can be covered.

Available deductibles are usually 5%, 10%, 15% and possibly 20%.

Commercial Earthquake Coverage

Earthquake coverage is also available for commercial properties. Very often commercial properties are built at least in part of masonry, which makes the cost of earthquake protection skyrocket. Masonry is more likely to suffer damage than wooden frame structures due to its rigidity and subsequent brittleness.

Earthquakes in the recent past have completely destroyed brick buildings and unreinforced masonry walls.

It was interesting to see the row of unreinforced cinder block walls all lying flat on the ground after the 1994 Northridge earthquake in California, although the owners I'm sure found it less than interesting. Building codes were changed just after that to require reinforcement with rebar.

The governing documents of Homeowner Associations may require earthquake coverage. Deductibles on a per-building basis are preferred, as it makes the deductible more manageable. If only one building is damaged in an earthquake, for example (very unlikely, but for illustrative purposes let's go with it,) that building's owners do not have to absorb the deductible for the entire complex, only the deductible for their building.

Unit owners should obtain personal earthquake coverage and make sure that the earthquake loss assessment coverage on their policy should concur with their potential loss assessment.

Chapter Summary/Key Takeaways

This type of coverage requires careful tailoring to make sure that adequate coverage is obtained and budgets are considered. This is definitely not a one size fits all type of coverage.

Chapter Seven: Health Insurance

This is a big one. It has been a political football for a few years now, due to the inclusion of certain features such as preexisting conditions, maternity and inclusion of children living in the household up to age 26. And I have to admit I am pretty opinionated on this one, but it is too long a conversation for this book. I will stick to the overview.

Health insurance comes in two basic flavors. HMO and PPO. Here is the essence.

HMO: This one is very popular with many people because it takes a lot of the decision-making out of their hands, and let's face it, most people are not medical savvy.

You choose a medical group that has a number of doctors affiliated with it. They may have a pediatrician, a gynecologist, a general medical doctor and maybe some others. They may all be in a single medical group building, or they may have their own offices.

There are also Hospitals associated with the group.

The insurance company takes in premium, gives a portion to the medical group that you have selected and does all of the medical billing and tracking. The medical group gets a monthly premium for being there for you.

When you need a doctor, you call the group and they put you in touch with the primary physician, who is called the "gatekeeper." That doctor will probably see you first and then decide if you will go to a specialist, and if there is no specialist in the group, the gatekeeper will decide if the group will pay for an outside specialist or a second opinion. They pay out of their pocket for that.

Your job is to find a group that has the doctor or doctors that you like and the hospital that you like. Then you sign up with that group under the insurance company you have chosen.

An HMO gets paid when you don't come in to see them. When you do come in to see them, you are now using their time and money. Now you are seeing my bias.

PPO: this is a different type of medical care. They only get paid when you come in to see them. There is no gatekeeper. You go to the doctor of your choice in the "network." That doctor will be affiliated with a particular hospital or hospitals, so there are some choices there for you.

If you do go to a provider in the PPO network, there will be some costs. There will be a deductible, which has to be met before the insurance company pays out. There is a sharing percentage, (maybe you will pay 20% of the cost of a visit or hospital stay) and an out of pocket maximum. It depends on the program you purchase. There is no doubt that this is a more expensive type of program, however, you get to choose your doctor, your specialist, your second opinion and your hospital, and you get to pay more for a PPO than an HMO. But you have choices.

You can even go out of network, but there is a different fee schedule for that, and it will cost you more out of pocket.

There is another option called an EPO (exclusive provider network,) which does not allow you to go outside the network at all—they won't pay for any of it. You may, however like the doctors in network, so it does not matter.

So, one type gets paid until you come in, and the other gets paid only when you come in. Your choice.

Chapter Eight: Life Insurance

Life Insurance for Individuals

Life insurance is an extremely versatile coverage. it can be used for family protection, savings, business protection, funding a trust and others. Let's take this one aspect at a time.

Types of life insurance include whole life, universal life and term life. You could divide them into two categories; term and permanent.

Whole life insurance is the original type of permanent coverage. It is a policy that promises a certain amount of benefit to a given beneficiary at a constant premium. It cannot be canceled unless you cancel it by not paying or by directive. It normally runs until you are age 99 and then you get all of your money back. It has a savings component that compounds the invested money at a guaranteed (although not very high) rate.

It is useful when you need a guaranteed premium over its lifetime for a guaranteed benefit, such as funding a trust, which will someday pay out the benefits with known tax consequences to pay inheritance taxes, gifts, build a hospital wing and other such uses.

Term life insurance is pretty much the direct opposite. The term is selected, as is the benefit amount based upon one's need for family protection while a family is growing, or a home is being paid off. The coverage ends when the term ends. More accurately, when the term ends, the premium goes up too high to keep the policy in force. You get forced out of the policy.

With a pure term policy, the rate begins low and increases as you age, in response to mortality rates (chance that you will die at any given age.) Most term currently written is level term, where the premiums are averaged over the term years, based on current mortality rates for each age. That way the premium remains level until the term ends and it all goes crazy. Typical terms are 10, 20 and 30 years. Premiums vary with the amount of coverage being purchased. $250,000 of coverage is one fourth of the cost of $1,000,00 of coverage, unless there are premium breaks for larger amounts.

Generally speaking, term premiums cost a fraction of the cost of whole life policy premiums, because with whole life, the insurance company is sure you will die, and they will have to pay out on the policy. Not necessarily so on a term life policy which may cancel before you die. You might say they are betting you will live, and they don't have to pay out. Morbid, yes?

Universal Life policies are a sort of hybrid. The premium inside the policy increases as with a pure term policy. The rates are calculated based on a certain number of years that you might keep the policy, and there is also a savings component with a guaranteed rate and a projected rate. This is used in the calculation to project how much money needs to go into the savings portion in order to offset the pure premium for any given number of years.

This type of policy comes with illustrations of both projections, and much care should be used before buying this type of policy. It is easy for agents to want to create more favorable projections in order to make a sale. That said, if done correctly, this is the most versatile type of permanent insurance. The savings portion can even be an investment product if sold by a properly licensed investment consultant.

Life Insurance for Business

Life insurance for business can be used to:

1. keep a valuable employee (designate that the policy you paid for will be his if he stays on,)

2. pay the company for the loss of a valuable employee (called key person coverage,)

3. buy out a partner's spouse if he dies,

4. have the corporation buy back an owner's stock, and other things.

It can be extremely useful if an agent is knowledgeable and has a competent legal and tax team behind him.

All life insurance policies are underwritten; which means that risk factors are taken into account. These can be obesity, smoking, hypertension, diabetes, medications taken, cholesterol level, lifestyle choices such as motorcycle racing and so on. The rates reflect those factors and can be significant. For example, we just quoted a term policy with and without smokers rating. The nonsmoker premium quote was one third the amount for the smoker rating.

Sometimes the risk factors are too high to qualify an applicant for any sort of coverage. I have had marijuana smokers, at-risk HIV applicants, obese people and heart disease applicants denied. A smart agent will know which insurance companies have the most lenient underwriting rules for a given medical issue.

Here is a caveat, though. Suppose you would like to game the system, and you misrepresent a material fact on an application. When it comes time for a claim to be paid, the contract becomes null and void. All your premiums will be returned and no benefits will be paid out.

This goes for all insurance policies, but in particular, life insurance.

Retirement from a Business

Most business owners think of retiring from the business at some point. They have worked very hard to get the business to the point where it now is, and it's time to kick back a little and work on the golf game.

How do you get out of your business when it's time?

Let's say you have been in business for some time, and family does not want to run the business when you are out. You have invested too much effort and time into making this business a success. Plus, you would like to earn some sort of residual when you let it go.

I suppose you could just sell the business. Aren't there plenty of potential buyers who would pay top dollar for your business? Probably not; every buyer is looking to steal, not buy.

Suppose you have an employee who would make an excellent business owner for your business, and you might really want him or her to take it over when you are done. Big problem, though, that employee will never be able to afford it when the time comes. What is to be done?

With a correctly structured program you could plan the buyout and the financing, and at the same time provide an incentive for her to stay on until that day when she takes over. You could even make it tax deductible. Believe it or not, business life insurance could come to the rescue.

You could, for example, structure a life insurance program in such a way that any savings within the policy could be available to purchase the business at some point, or at least offer a sufficient down payment to get it going. There are options as to ownership and payment, and of course tax benefits.

Life insurance, disability insurance and annuities are vehicles that allow for some very creative ways of protecting an existing business, keeping an employee of value, planning for a future sale, rewarding an employee of value, and other things. The capabilities change along with the changes in existing tax laws, so advantages come and go with time. Further exploration with a life insurance agent who has an available legal department is critical. Most life insurance agents are not prepared to have this discussion, as they are focused on family protection life insurance. This type of coverage is as different as night is to day and requires a special subset of skills and training as an agent.

Here is another scenario. Imagine a partner, a stockholder on a small company or a managing member in an LLC dies. The solutions are similar to those discussed in the Disability Insurance section, but life insurance is the vehicle.

Chapter Summary/Key Takeaways

Life Insurance is an extremely versatile form of coverage. Get with the right type of agent and be able to solve a myriad of problems.

We mentioned disability insurance. Let's have a closer look in the next chapter.

Chapter Nine: Disability Insurance

Personal Disability Insurance

Just suppose that you are a working person and you get disabled and can't work. There is a coverage for you that can supplement your state disability coverage and really protect you. Disability insurance would pay you while you didn't work. The amount they pay us usually 65% of your regular pay (they don't want you to stay on disability coverage forever, so they don't pay the full amount of your paycheck.) You can select the elimination period (how long until you start getting paid,) the term of payment (long term or short term,) and there are add-ons such as keeping up with the cost of living, partial disability payments and more. Each of these has an effect on the premium.

There are some other factors such as guaranteed renewable (premium can go up,) and non-cancellable (premium can't go up nor can the benefits be reduced.) The type of work done and the other parameters above will affect premium, as will health.

Disability Insurance for Business

Imagine that there are two or three other good friends who are all pretty competent in business, but they decide that a partnership between them all would make for a successful new business. So, they all get together and form a partnership or a corporation and start a business.

Things go along just fine until one of the partners gets sick or becomes disabled. Then the questions arise.

Who is going to hold up his or her end of the business?

Is that partner married? Wow! Now you are in business with a spouse, and if that spouse is not contributing to the business, he or she is still getting paid and have basically a free ride. Is that fair to the business?

What if the spouse is liked personally, but not as a business partner? That could be even worse, and could end a successful, ongoing business.

Business disability can be structured to assure the remaining partners, corporate shareholders or managing members that the business will go on, mostly as designed, but without the former partner's spouse interfering. That spouse could be bought out and walk away happy and feel well cared for.

A sole proprietor could buy a business disability policy to protect his ongoing overhead if he/she is unable to work the business for a while. This can also be put in place for a key employee, where either the business gets replacement income for the absent employee or the employee gets replacement income while not working, or both.

The same types of features and underwriting exist as for individual disability coverage.

Chapter Summary/Key Takeaways

This type of coverage also requires an agent who specializes. If you need business disability coverage, do find a company who has a large "back room" with tax lawyers and other specialists.

Let's explore business insurance coverage in the next part.

Part III: Business Insurance

Chapter Ten: How to Read a Business Insurance Policy

Navigating an insurance policy can be a daunting thing. You just received your policy from your agent and you would really like to know what it says on that 50 to 100 pages of text and form.

I can explain how a policy is structured. I won't go into specifics about the coverages in this article, but you will at least have a roadmap as to where the various parts are, and what they try to do.

I specialize in commercial insurance, and so I will dedicate a whole part to that topic and how it varies with different types of business.

Disclosures

Lately it seems that the disclosure section of a policy comes before the informational section. Many policies are including 20 to 40 pages of disclosures. Information on Terrorism coverage, Flood coverage, employee characterization, coverage changes from prior year, and updates to coverage. How to file claims may also be stated in those pages. This information used to be disclosed at the back of the policy, and you could get straight to the meat of your particular policy coverages, but disclosures have taken over. In any case, you may find that those pages come first and you will have to plough through them before you get to the information about your specific policy.

Declaration Pages

These show the summary of your coverage amounts, dates of your coverage, who is insuring you, and the cost of insurance. This page or pages are what are termed "Declaration Pages," and are actually required by law to have the above descriptions and information. They disclose to you all in one place what you are paying for when you buy a policy.

Another section of the Declarations page has a list of the forms and endorsements to the policy. More on this later. In all, these pages can be from 1 to 10 or more in number, depending on how much detail is in them. Whereas most of the policy will be boiler plate, these pages specify how your coverage is written. Coverages can be broken down by type and location. You will often see the rating base of the policy on these pages. That will tell you how they arrived at your premium.

Rating Base

To digress just a bit, the rating base of a policy is how the premium was achieved. There may be a rate for area, gross sales, property amount, payroll, or other rating bases depending on what type of business is being insured. The rate used is multiplied against the rating base, or amount, in order to get the premium for that portion of the total premium. For example, you might have a rating base of $8.68 per $1000 of gross sales.

Classification Number

Along with the rating base is a classification number, not always shown in the declarations page. This number is critical, as it defines which rate is to be used. Mathematicians who are called actuaries for insurance purposes use statistics from past losses for each type of business to determine the possibility of future losses. They also take into account other factors, such as their tolerance for risk or how much they can realistically charge for a classification, as well as what they think the future may hold in terms of marketplace, weather in the case of Flood coverage, and so on.

The insurance companies then use the actuarial information and assign their own rate to the classification number. Then they have to file that rate with the insurance department. And if the insurance department disagrees, they can disallow that rate from being used.

In any case, the classification may be on display for you to see how the insurance company arrived at your rate.

Double Check Your Premium

If you see a rate that doesn't calculate out correctly, it could be that despite the premium coming out at one amount, you are being charged a higher rate, it could be that you are subject to a "minimum premium." This is the lowest premium for which the insurance company will sell the policy, despite the rating factors.

And by the way, this is one of the reasons that it is important to shop insurance coverage; one company may have a greater tolerance for your type of business's risk factors than another, and we could get a lower premium.

Insurance Forms

So back on track: next come the insurance forms with standardized wording. Some insurance companies use wording standardized by the Insurance Services Office (ISO.) Technically speaking, the ISO provides *statistical, actuarial, underwriting, and claims information and analytics; compliance and fraud identification tools; policy language; information about specific locations; and technical services.*

The language used should be plain, understandable English. That does not mean that it may not need some interpretation. And some parts refer back to earlier parts. It reminds me of a French cookbook I once used. I was ready to prepare a dish on page 253, when it told me to use the beef stock described on page 40, which they assumed I had prepared earlier and had sitting around. I don't cook French anymore.

ISO wording is used by most insurance companies, and if you see their designation at the bottom of a form, you know it has been standardized. This is a good thing, because when you compare coverages from different companies, if they are using ISO forms, you are comparing apples to apples. On the other hand, if an insurance company uses its own wording, you may not know what is included or excluded, as you can't compare it to standard. This is called "manuscript wording" and there are many companies who do use it. It is not necessarily a bad thing, but you have to select your insurance company carefully and analyze the wording.

Property Forms

Usually the property forms come first after the declaration pages. Sometimes they are preceded by a rating page. The property form will define the types of property covered, how thoroughly it is covered, where it is covered, under what perils it is covered, and under what conditions. Exclusions are also noted in this section, and should be examined, so you know what is not covered. Included is a section on how losses are paid.

After the property section, you will see a number of endorsements. These either enhance the standard wording or are exclusion wording that clarifies what is not covered. These types of endorsements are often added by purchase to enhance coverage, or you can purchase the deletion of an exclusion.

General Liability

The section on commercial general liability usually comes after property. Liability protects you from lawsuit in the event that you hurt someone's body or property. It also defines the personal injury which may be covered; libel slander, false arrest, false imprisonment, wrongful eviction, and the like.

There is a section on who is an insured; the insured, family, employees, and so on. There is a section on what will be the responsibility of the insurance company and also a section on what is included and what is excluded.

Just as with property coverage, the liability section may be preceded by a rating page, and after the forms, there are endorsements which can either enhance or limit coverage under certain conditions. Again, in some cases you can pay to buy enhancements or to make limitations go away.

You may ask why there are endorsements. Good question. A standard policy form is a basic wording that may be used for many different types of businesses, anything from apartment buildings to plumbing contractors. Each of these businesses has different needs and ways of operating, and the endorsements tailor the basic wording to specific businesses so that you don't need a different form for each type of wording.

Chapter Eleven: Business Property and Coinsurance

Trying to save money by insuring for less?

Let's think this through. This concept will apply to business property insurance, which, for a small business can be pricey. There is therefore a temptation to insure for less than the actual replacement value of your business property. Sure, why not? I will never lose all of my business property. If there is a theft, it will only involve some property and I have enough coverage for that amount. That is definitely not how property insurance works. There is a clause called a coinsurance clause which, stated simply is "if you insure for half, you will be paid half, even in case of a partial loss. This situation could come back to haunt you.

Here is the process in more detail:

If you have $100,000 of inventory and fixtures, but you want to save a few dollars on the insurance, you may be tempted to insure, say, $25,000 of it and call it a day. The chances are slim that you would lose it all in one incident, right? My example comes from a true story, and I hope it motivates you to always "insure to value," and review annually.

I had a client who insured his office contents for $25,000, which included both property, and fixtures installed by him. Every year, I would ask him if the coverage was correct, and he would assure me that it was. One night, on a New Year's Eve, as it turned out, he had a burglary, where his proprietary computer system was stolen. The total loss was about $40,000. So, did he receive the full $25,000 for which he was covered? No, he did not.

The assumption with insurance is that an insured will insure to value. If you have $100,000, you insure that much, otherwise, you only get partial coverage.

As it turned out, he should have been insuring for about $75,000. He insured for one third of value, and since property coverages have a coinsurance clause, he got paid one third of his partial loss, minus his deductible. This, even though he had more coverage than that. In my client's case, he received $25,000 divided by $75,000, less deductible; about $8000, on his $40,000 loss.

For those of you who are more mathematically inclined, the formula is as follows:

Actual insured amount divided by the amount it should have been insured for, times the Actual loss, then subtract the deductible.

As you can see, even a partial loss will not be paid in full if not insured in full.

The moral is to insure to value. And don't depend on your insurance agent to read your mind. You must inform your agent of any changes to operations, management, inventory, fixtures or anticipated receipts and payroll. Do it when you have the changes, so you won't forget.........better yet, do it before it happens so your agent can anticipate any possible repercussions. And do it in writing. Send a copy of the email to yourself and keep it on file.

Chapter Twelve: Admitted, Non-Admitted, Surplus

You may have run into these terms if you have been looking for liability coverage. What are they all about?

Here in California, we have two types of insurance companies. Admitted and non-admitted.

Admitted

Admitted insurance carriers are approved by the state to do business. They are subject to audit and must join the state guarantee fund, a sort of safety net which would pay for any unpaid claims if the company becomes insolvent. Interestingly, these are generally very large companies with lots of assets and can afford the costs involved with being admitted in California. And not incidentally, they are unlikely to go insolvent due to their size.

Admitted carriers are the ones you mostly hear about. They are large and they advertise. They are household names. They appoint agents and brokers directly if they are promised a certain minimum amount of business and sometimes require exclusivity.

Non-Admitted

Non-admitted carriers are less well known unless you are in certain trades. Their policies are sold through wholesalers and surplus lines brokers. Some are very large, and in fact may be a subsidiary of an admitted carrier. Others are smaller and some are very small. They provide insurance for riskier types of policies. They normally have a much lower volume of business than admitted carriers, so the wholesaler may offer many different non-admitted carriers in order to satisfy a number of needs.

Non-admitted carriers do not offer the protection of the state guarantee fund, so it is important that the surplus lines carrier selected to write a policy is thoroughly researched as to financial strength. That way they are less likely to go insolvent, leaving claims on the table. In the late 1990s when the workers comp marketplace suffered a depression as many carriers went insolvent, leaving claims unpaid.

Sometimes the lines cross between admitted and non-admitted. For example, I was referred a plumbing contractor, for whom I submitted applications to the usual surplus lines companies. Then I discovered that there are two admitted companies who might take on a plumber with low receipts, new in business, no track record, and so on. You never know if such markets exist unless you have access to many, many markets.

When you purchase a non-admitted policy through a surplus lines wholesaler, there is a disclosure to sign. It is written in bold, all capital letters, warning the purchaser that they are buying a non-admitted policy and there are risks of claims going unpaid.

The A.M. Best company is a rating bureau most often used to evaluate financial strength of a carrier and is a good source for researching a carrier's credentials. A carrier must pay to be audited, and some very small carriers may choose not to be audited.

The state of California offers a LESLI list (list of eligible surplus lines insurers) of approved non-admitted carriers who are likely good prospects. They have had state audits and are recommended as a viable alternative to admitted carriers.

The state wants to make sure you select an admitted carrier when at all possible, so they require documentation that your agent has done a diligent search prior to offering you a non-admitted carrier's policy as an option.

In general, though there is nothing to be feared if your business can only be insured through a non-admitted insurance carrier, if it is a quality carrier.

Chapter Thirteen: General Liability Coverage

If you have ever wondered how the insurance company arrives at a premium quote for your business, you will want to read further.

The first thing to note is that not all insurance policies have ratable general liability coverage. If the general liability risk is low or pretty standardized for a particular type of business, a BOP, or "Business Owners Package," may be available for that business. There are a number of types of business that qualify for a BOP; for example, an office, a retail store or an apartment building.

However, if your business is one whose liability risk is dependent on several factors, your premium may have to be calculated. Here are rating factors that affect your general Liability risk.

Class of Business:

Different businesses have different risk factors, so the insurance industry has set up a rating system for different types of businesses. Contractors, for example, are riskier to insure than electrical circuit board assemblers. And even within the contractor world, there are different risk factors. A contractor who specializes in framing new construction buildings would be riskier than one who installs carpeting.

Let's explore why. Rates always come down to how much the insurance company could lose if you had a claim. If a framing job is not done correctly, a home could be flimsier, and subject to moving and shaking under normal circumstances (don't think earthquake.) If a completed house moves, it causes plumbing, tile, flooring and other items to be damaged, so the extent of the financial (and possibly the physical) damage might be costlier. And since the insurance company is responsible for covering damages for about a 10-year period, the statute of limitations on a claim, they are on the hook for a long time. A bad framing job could cause a million-dollar home to require extensive remodeling.

Couldn't happen? Think about this scenario. If a builder is in a hurry, or running short on cash, he might be inclined to drive nails into studs every 12 inches instead of every 6 inches. The county inspector may miss that upon approving the job. This has actually happened during my experience when a tract of condos was going up very quickly. Time is money to a builder.

So, the insurance industry has developed classes for each type of contractor, based upon their perceived riskiness to insure. Each class will have a rate attached to it by each individual insurance carrier who wants to write that type of business.

Audits:

While we are talking about rating factors, it is important to select a quote with the lowest possible rate, because at the end of the year, an audit will be done. When a policy is written, the insured estimates the amount of the factors by which his premium is calculated—called a rating base. If his rate is $5.00 per $1000 of payroll, his initial quote might be for $500,000 of gross sales, and his premium might then be $2500. At the end of the year, the carrier reviews the actual gross sales and adjusts for that. So, if you estimated $500,000 but sold $800,000, the carrier will come back at the end of the year and ask for another $1500.

Can't happen? One of my recent clients estimated $1,000,000 of sales, but due to clever marketing, actually sold $15,000,000 of services. Great for him, but the audit wanted an additional $60,000. Ouch!!

So how does the insurance company decide on their rates?

Industry Loss Information:

Insurance companies are extremely good at using numbers and statistics; far better than any baseball analyst. Loss information for each class and subclass of business are available by location and other factors. This allows prediction of anticipated losses. From that, their actuaries calculate what rates should be charged for a class of business.

Actuaries are mathematicians who work for insurance companies for the specific purpose of predicting future losses based on past losses and other factors.

The insurance carrier has to file their rates with the insurance department. They have to stick to those rates until the next annual filing, when their rating decision might change. They also file a credit structure, which allows them to mitigate the rates for a particular risk (remember that term?)

Credits:

There are mitigating factors to the rates. Rates have some leeway based upon credits that can be applied by the underwriter. The underwriter is the one who evaluates the application for insurance from a particular business, and decides whether to quote the coverage at all, or to write it, or how to rate it. If the underwriter applies credits to mitigate the applied rate, he or she must justify that credit with some notation about how well the business is maintained, how much experience the business owner has, and other information. They try to get to know the particular business so that they can apply the best rate possible and win the business away from other quotes that might have been offered by other insurance carriers.

There are other rating factors as well.

Prior Business Losses.

When quoting a particular business insurance, the underwriter will ask for "loss runs." These are a declaration of losses experienced by the current and prior insurance carriers who covered this business. They will detail the amount paid out on each particular loss. The obtained loss runs should go back five years. They must be on the letterhead of the insurance carrier who covered the business for those years. They must also have been procured within 90 days of the renewal date of the current policy or of the quote.

Why 90 days and not last year's loss runs? How often have I seen claims closed, reopened, or new claims appear even after 5 years! The loss runs must be "fresh" in order to be accurate.

- If a business has only two years of experience, they won't have five years of loss runs, and this can affect the credits applied.
- If the loss runs show many small losses, a large loss, or particular types of losses for that type of business, that will affect credits, and sometimes whether the underwriter even wants to offer a quote.
- If an underwriter is not familiar with a particular type of business, you may not get a good quote. It could be up to the broker to "educate" the underwriter as to what the business does.

While we are discussing the broker's role, I have gotten better quotes by assuring the underwriter when I have had a client for five, ten or twenty years, in some cases; or I know the family, or I have other types of business with the owner, or other signs of familiarity. Brokers have to know their underwriters, and underwriters have to know the brokers well enough to trust them. If an underwriter has no faith in the broker because the broker lied in order to push through a particular piece of business before, then this quote may be a difficult one to get.

Website.

Everyone has a website now, and on the website, we brag about our capabilities. This helps us get business in the door. But…..if the website has information on it that is not on the application, there could be a problem. If a nail salon claims only to do nails, but their website says they do eyebrow waxing, or worse yet, Brazilian waxing, the underwriter will not like it. Waxing is considerably riskier than doing nails and is more likely to cause a lawsuit. That's bad. Can't happen? Did happen. Every example in this writing comes from something in my own experience.

Newsflash!!! Underwriters ask for your website URL so they can double check what you do. If it does not match your application, they will ask for clarification. They may ask you to remove wording which you say does not reflect what you do. "I had it on the website because I thought I might do some waxing, but I haven't done any, and I won't do any." Take it off the website in order to avoid underwriting problems.

The underwriter has a certain degree of discretion. If they are uncertain, you may not get any quote at all. If you add a service during the policy year that they don't like, your policy may get "non-renewed." If everything is good, you may get a great quote.

More influencing factors:

- An insurance carrier's overall loss experience -
  1. The insurance carrier's overall loss experience for a certain type of business. I was a direct agent for an insurance company before I became a broker. One year they decided they wanted to write coverage for wholesale distributors. And they developed very aggressive pricing. So, we developed marketing programs to attract and write wholesale distributors.

The very next year, that company decided that writing wholesale distributors was not profitable for them, so they non-renewed all of the distributors I had worked so hard to write business for. Not profitable means that they underestimated the losses compared to the attainable premium for that type of business class.

- Reinsurance cost -

2. Behind the insurance marketplace is a secondary marketplace called the reinsurance market. There are companies that you have never heard of who invest in risk and sell that risk. This is somewhat like the secondary loan market, which buys up large lots of loans at a discount, so that lenders can free up money with which to make more loans. It works the same for insurance. Carriers might sell off chunks of risk at a discount in order to free up money with which to offer more insurance policies. The law requires that insurers have assets in a large proportion compared to the policies they hold. If reinsurance becomes more expensive, or unattainable, or the insurance company runs out of cash this year before they can purchase more "risk" from the reinsurance market, which may only open up next year, they may turn away business by quoting high. If a business is desperate and wants to buy high, the carrier may will take it; otherwise, they won't.

- Market Pressure -

3. An insurance carrier may decide to price aggressively because it needs to put business on the books. It may be that they are an existing company exploring a new market, or a company positioning themselves for a takeover or purchase. They may believe they will make it up in future years with higher and higher pricing. Also, the first year that an insurance product is offered, there are no losses to pay out, so it can be cheaper. Once there are losses, they have to look at both aspects of their P&L statement; profits, vs. losses.

- Your preference -

4. You may want or need the pricier policy. It may have features that you require. Or the carrier may be financially stronger and you feel more comfortable with them. You may prefer an admitted insurance carrier

because of the financial protection of the state guarantee fund that stands behind it, as compared with a non-admitted carrier, which does not participate in that program. The state guarantee fund is similar to the FDIC, which protects your money in case of bank failure. It protects you in the event of insurance company failure and inability to pay claims. If that were to happen, you get to pay the claims.

All of these considerations go into the pricing of a liability policy. Where you fall in the pricing structure depends on your track record and on your carrier's track record, as well as a number of other variables.

Chapter Fourteen: Commercial Vehicle Insurance

Why do I want commercial vehicle insurance anyhow? Why can't I just insure my trucks under my personal policy? Let's address that very question.

There are two major ways in which one can insure a vehicle used for business, depending on the actual use, the type of vehicle and the insurance company.

Personal Auto Insurance, generally speaking, covers your vehicle while going to and from work and for personal use. Sales use may also be allowed.

Commercial Auto Insurance: covers your vehicle for business use, which can be sales, service or commercial trucking. Personal auto policies actually exclude most types of business use.

Let's take a closer look at the uses themselves.

Sales use: this is called business use on a personal auto policy. It assumes that mileage you put on your vehicle will be for traveling to customers' sites to make sales, speak to existing clients, go to meetings or meals with clients and so on. This could be use in a private passenger vehicle or a pickup truck up to half-ton. Not all personal lines companies will allow this category.

Such a policy will be rated for business use and covered that way. Beware of using your personal vehicle for sales calls and not advising your insurer that you are doing that, as your policy may specifically exclude such use unless endorsed for business. Your insurance carrier may not even allow such endorsements, and you don't want any rude surprises in case of an accident.

Make sure that if you are driving for work, that you have adequate insurance coverage. $30,000/$60,000 will not do if you are in business. An accident in your business vehicle will likely exceed that limit, and then they go after the business. Get the highest limits you can.

Service Use: An example of this would be a contractor using a pickup truck to go to a work site or sites, where he would be using his tools for his job. You don't even have to think contractor in this. You could just as easily think domestic cleaning service, such as a maid service. The maids (actually janitorial workers,) go from customer to customer during the day and do their work in each location, bringing their cleaning tools with them. We can think of other examples as well.

Commercial use: an example would be delivering packages, or products such as raw materials. The type of vehicle used could be a personal vehicle like a minivan delivering printed products, to a step van such as FedEx or UPS, all the way up to a gasoline truck, cement truck, tow truck or produce truck. Heavy equipment qualifies as commercial use as well. Think tractor and trailer or flatbed. As long as it can be registered to travel on roads and freeways, it can be commercial use. Equipment such as bulldozers are in a different category.

So why bother with commercial insurance at all?

Your client may require you to have certain coverages not afforded by personal insurance.

Your client may require higher limits than available on a personal insurance policy; $1,000,000 for example. Personal lines policies normally do not have limits this high.

Your client may require an additional insured certificate, which actually names them as part of your policy. This is very common with commercial, and largely unavailable for personal lines.

You may need to tow a commercial trailer. This is definitely not covered by personal lines insurance.

You may have employees who drive for work incidentally (running to the Post Office for stamps,) or consistently (a salesman using her personal vehicle to make sales for your company.) For this type of use, you would add non-owned auto coverage to your policy. This protects your business in the event that this person is in an accident while on company time or business.

This coverage can actually save a business. I did have a client who asked an employee to pick up something for the business owner, and the driver got into an accident. Of course, if an attorney finds out that it is business use, they will sue the business for any damages, and if you are using a personal policy for business use, you will not be covered and the business will lose. If you are operating your business as an individual rather than as a corporation or LLC, such a lawsuit can affect your personal life and assets directly.

If you are in business, the best protection for you is to operate under an entity such as an LLC or a corporation and insure your vehicles under that entity.

Chapter Fifteen: EPLI; I Was Only Kidding

Is that your defense, Mr. Jones?

"I was only kidding"; "it didn't happen like that"; "it was consensual"; "she wanted it"; "it was no big deal"; "I'm innocent"; and the ever popular, "I'm old and blind."

What the heck is going on in the world? Employers are feeling like this is a game of whack a mole with employee issues. One gets solved, the next one pops up. Even Google employees took a full day to walk off the job in protest—by the thousands—all over the world. What has happened to our world?

This apparently is not something new. What is new is the social media interaction that allows people to realize that they are not the only one with a problem of being harassed. That gives them strength to come forward, possibly even some opportunistic situations, but likely not, in most cases.

Employees have become aware that there are workplace issues and are beginning to take action. They are too sensitive, you say? It's innocent and they should suck it up? Unfortunately, that seems to be a genie that will never return to the bottle. From here forward, the rules have changed in the workplace, and employers will just have to deal with it.

For years, workers compensation carriers have required that employee handbooks be in place, and that they cover employee interactions. Very often, the rules were not observed. Now the game has changed.

Employers will now have to be ever so much more cautious about creating a workplace that is safe and treats everyone equally. That goes for men as well as women. I personally know of a situation where a married male friend of mine was sexually pressured by his supervisor, also a male. This ultimately caused a mental breakdown of my friend. At the time, 30 years ago, there was no recourse for him, but to quit a really good aerospace job.

Even if you are an employer who runs a "clean shop," treats everyone well, and makes sure that nothing unseemly happens between employees in his business, he may still be accused by a disgruntled employee for something that is not the case. The ensuing reputation damage and legal costs could break the bank. I have personally seen this scenario. What is to be done?

There is an insurance coverage that has been around for more than 20 years, called Employment Practices Liability Insurance; EPLI. My agency has been writing this coverage for years, but many employers have not wanted to step up and purchase it, because they felt that their house was clean and nothing could happen. "look, nothing has happened in all these years; why would it now?" That could be the very definition of "famous last words."

As a result of social media, people are more aware now, and that is making it far more likely that something will happen going forward.

So, what is EPLI coverage? It has a number of coverages that span many areas. Here is a partial list:

- violation of any federal, state, local or common law, prohibiting any kind of employment-related discrimination.

- harassment, including any type of sexual or gender harassment as well as racial, gender, religious, national origin, sexual orientation or preference, transgender status, pregnancy, disability (including HIV), marital or family status, mental status, age, obesity, genetic information or predisposition (including BRCA status) - based harassment and including harassment via **Social Media** and workplace harassment by non-employees;

- abusive or hostile work environment;

- workplace bullying;

- wrongful discharge or termination of employment, whether actual or constructive;

- breach of an implied employment contract, breach of the implied covenant of good faith and fair dealing, or promissory estoppel;

- breach of an actual or alleged written employment contract as long as another **Wrongful Employment Practice** is also alleged;

- wrongful failure or refusal to hire or promote, or wrongful demotion;

- wrongful failure or refusal to provide equal treatment or opportunities;

- employment termination, disciplinary action, demotion or other employment decision that violates public policy or the Family Medical Leave Act or similar state or local law;

- defamation, libel, slander, disparagement, false imprisonment, misrepresentation, malicious prosecution, or invasion of privacy;

- wrongful failure or refusal to adopt or enforce adequate grievance policies or procedures;

- wrongful, excessive or unfair discipline;

- wrongful infliction of emotional distress, mental anguish, or humiliation;

- Privacy Violation

- retaliation, including retaliation for exercising protected rights, supporting in any way another's exercise of protected rights, or threatening or actually reporting wrongful activity of an **Insured** such as violation of any federal, state, or local "whistle blower" law;

- wrongful deprivation of career opportunity with the **Insured Company**, negligent evaluation or failure to grant tenure;

- improper use of background checks in any employment decision to hire, fire, discipline, promote or demote;

- violation of the Uniformed Services Employment and Reemployment Rights Act or other federal, state or local statute protecting the reemployment of military personnel; or

- negligent hiring or negligent supervision of others, including wrongful failure to provide adequate training, in connection with 1 through 19 above,

- **Employment Event Loss**

- **"Employment Event"** means any of the following events, which shall be deemed to commence (i) when an executive officer of the **Insured Company** first believes in good faith that it is more likely than not that such event will occur within the next sixty (60) days, or (ii) with respect to 5. below, when the event occurs, whichever is earlier:

And there is more, but the above list is enough to strike fear into the strongest employer and have them wonder if it is all worth it.

What is also covered is the cost of legal fees, so an employer can protect herself if accused.

How much does this all cost? At one time it was less costly than it is now, but since the two famous Hollywood cases from the recent past, the cost has risen along with the likelihood that more employers could have disgruntled employees. And surprisingly, they seem to come out of the woodwork when a lawsuit is filed.

Is it worth it? As with all insurance, it's much cheaper to insure than it is to pay out of pocket once there is a lawsuit.

Chapter Sixteen: Professional Liability

More and more, the US has become a service economy and less of a manufacturing economy. That means that we are providing more services rather than product. Some of those services are in the form of advice, and as such, wrong advice can cause harm to those we advise.

So, who might be providers of advice?

Certainly, those in the insurance business. Add to those the ones in the legal profession. Include other advisory professions such as accountants, architects, consultants, lenders, realtors, certain programmers, cyber technologists, and more. The list is very long. Don't forget the medical and dental professions, although their wrongly provided service is called "malpractice," as opposed to just advice.

There are two rough categories of harm that can be caused by incorrect service; financial and physical. A financial advisor may cause financial harm by his error or his omission. Financial compensation might be sought from such a case. On the other hand, if an architect does a poor job in design, his design may result in collapse of a building, and harm to individuals and property (other than the property he designed.) A doctor might cause disease or loss of a limb due to an omission. Both of these examples could also result in financial loss.

You might wonder whether general liability coverage would cover such exposure.

General liability, after all, does protect the insured in case he is sued for bodily injury or property damage to a third party. General liability is not designed to cover poor advice or service, and so exclusions are specifically named such that the coverage does not go so far as providing protection against those and other exposures specifically covered by professional Liability.

Let's look at how insurance might offer a remedy.

What we now call "Professional Liability" coverage was once called E and O, which stands for Errors and Omissions. Stating the obvious, an insured could make an error in judgment and cause loss, or they might overlook a point that later becomes an issue.

The term "Professional Liability" is broader than just E&O, however. Over the years, such coverage as negligence, misrepresentation, violation of good faith and fair dealing, and inaccurate advice have been added to the basic E&O definition of coverage.

As an example of how a loss might occur, if a Trust attorney does not have experience on the possible outcomes of a particular type of wording, and she neglects to provide a clarification in a trust that she writes, property might not be properly protected, heirs may suffer losses to their inheritances, or the state may have to arbitrate an outcome; that process being lengthy and expensive to the heirs.

In addition, certain occupations have a component of physical loss exposure in addition to financial loss exposure. Architects for sure have that, as do Doctors. Certain consultants also have that. One of my clients' programs control computers for assembly robots and gantry cranes. If he programs one incorrectly and it drops a load onto someone or something, there would be both physical and financial damage. He has a type of professional liability program called Architects and Engineers coverage, which would cover both types of damage.

That consultant also has general liability coverage just in case he is at a client location and creates a physical hazard resulting in injury or financial loss, but not related to his programming. It is, in fact, General liability coverage.

As a side note, no insurance company will allow willful acts to be covered, so general and professional liability policies exclude willful or criminal acts. If it is shown, for example that the outcome of an action was known before the service was provided, that could be fraud. Fraud is criminal, and criminal acts are never covered by insurance contracts.

As another side note, sometimes the lines become blurred when speaking of prior knowledge. These often become decided in court as both sides argue whether or not there was prior knowledge. In fact, the exact time of loss, including prior knowledge leads us into the next aspect of Professional Liability coverage, and that is the coverage form.

What should one look for in a professional liability policy?

There is a clause called "duty to defend." If that clause is not there, then you may be on your own in defense of your position and only be reimbursed after a lengthy trial. Costly, to say the least.

There may be a window within which a claim must be filed; often 60 days from the time of notification of the event as an example. If the notification to the insurance company falls outside of that, the company may not have a "duty to defend."

Since these policies are almost always written on a "claims made" basis, there must be prior acts coverage, otherwise anything that happened prior to the effective date of this year's policy may not be covered—even if that policy is a continuation of the last year's policy. And don't let that policy lapse, or the prior acts coverage restarts with this year's effective date. Not a good scenario.

How much tail coverage is offered, and how much does it cost? Tail coverage is mentioned in the liability section.

Chapter Seventeen: Workers Compensation

If you have employees, you will need to buy workers compensation coverage to protect them. It does not matter if they work part time, some time or one time. The law says they must be protected from injury while they are doing work for you.

Oh, and if you think you can pay someone on a 1099, call him an independent contractor and not have to pay workers comp on him, you may be in for a surprise. There are specific guidelines for who is an independent contractor, and they are narrow. Just because he receives a 1099, he could still be an employee. Ask your agent for help on this one. It could cost you at audit time when actual payrolls are reviewed.

Workers Comp coverage pays wage replacement benefits and medical reimbursement if you are injured. It also pays disability payments and a small amount of death payment.

There are two main criteria for the amount that an employer might pay for his workers comp premium.

Firstly, there is a rate. Each type of job has a risk factor. Office workers have a lower risk factor than fire fighters. Companies evaluate their risk tolerance and ability to market to whichever segment of the business community they may want to approach. Not every company wants to write fire fighters, they may only want to write small retail businesses. Once the company determines its preferences, it files a base rate with the state and must stick to that rate. They may also file rate modification criteria which would give them a leeway of up to 25%, for example. If there is enough premium to warrant it, the workers comp bureau may also evaluate a particular business to see if its losses are better or worse than expected and then assign a modifier of its own, called an experience modification.

The rates are expressed as a number which is a factor per $100 of payroll. So, a rate of 5.00 might be applied to a payroll of $100,000 to get a raw rate of $5000 of premium. This rate might then be further modified up or down depending on the discounts and the experience modification. So, with a 25% discount applied by the insurance company and a 20% discount resulting from a good "x-mod" the premium would be $3000. If there are losses, you might lose the discount and have a 1.25 x-mod and pay $6250 instead.

If there is a poor loss record, a lapse in coverage or a type of business considered too risky for most workers comp companies, the court of last resort (in California) is the State Compensation Insurance Fund—SCIF.) Some states only have a SCIF and no private carriers. In any case, SCIF cannot decline to insure a company who wants coverage and complies with the requests, but they can charge and surcharge. Oh, Yes.

At the end of a policy year, the workers comp carrier will perform an audit. This makes sure that they charged the correct premium. They may ask for financial statements to show actual payrolls, or just ask for a simple form to be completed. If you underestimated payroll for the year, expect an invoice. If you overestimated, there will be a refund.

The employer must allow them to proceed with this audit process. If not, the carrier may want to make sure that your actual payroll was not more than your estimated payroll at the beginning of the policy period. So, they add 10% to 20% to the bill just to make sure. it's legal.

Avoiding claims is critical. Keeping a clean, uncluttered business location with an eye toward what can happen to cause injury is important. Having safety meetings is important. Safety communication with employees is important. Even then, employees do bonehead things and the employer is the one to suffer.

A client of mine had a machine shop with large presses which stamp down on pieces of metal in order to form them. According to standards, such machines are to have a number of safeguards. There must be a yellow line around the machine, within which only the operator is allowed to stand while working the machine. This is to prevent distractions.

Another safeguard is the placement of handholds out of the way of the machinery's working components, so that the machine will only operate when the operator's hands are clear of the press. If you are a machine operator in a hurry to produce your parts, you may be tempted to circumvent that safeguard. This particular operator taped the safety switch in place so he did not need to place his hands on it and out of the way of the press. His hand was in the way when the press came down. This resulted in a three-fingered operator, and a large workers compensation claim.

There are many other situations that can result in a claim, so safety should be top of mind for every employer, even those with only clerical staff. An employee can throw out her back by just bending or lifting incorrectly. Instruction on how to safely lift even lightweight items is important.

Chapter Eighteen: Garage Liability

Auto repair shops and auto body shops both have a unique situation where they are in charge of others' vehicles. They need general liability coverage AND they need coverage in case a vehicle in their charge gets damaged or stolen. They also have to drive vehicles from one area to another, and they have to test drive vehicles on the street.

Then there is the issue of business property, which may include tools and equipment belonging to the owner and also to the mechanics, who often have to purchase their own.

With respect to liability coverage, they need the usual general liability. Add to that they need auto liability coverage for when they drive a vehicle.

After that, there is a specific type of coverage called garage keepers liability. This is a type of bailee's coverage (coverage for others' property within your care, custody and control,) which protects the vehicles that a shop is working on. It comes in three flavors.

Garage Keepers legal liability: say a vehicle is stored overnight while being worked on. If it is burned down or vandalized, Garage Keepers Legal Liability will require that the garage keeper be deemed legally liable before insurance will pay. That often means an investigation, possibly a lawsuit, and you know that an insurance company will do what it can to show that the garage keeper was not liable so they don't have to pay.

Then there is Garage Keepers Direct Insurance. If it is Direct Excess, then it comes into play only after the vehicle owner's own comprehensive or collision coverage pays out. And they may not, because the vehicle was not under the owner's care and control at the time.

The best coverage is Garage Keepers Direct Primary, which pays out first without respect to the vehicle owner's coverage.

Garage Keepers Liability must cover all the vehicles in the shop, just in case. The application asks how many vehicles might be in the shop at a given time. the maximum number and the average number. and then, what is the average value of vehicles being worked on.

For years I insured a shop that specialized in Porsche automobiles. They did take in the occasional Jaguar or Mercedes, but always high-end vehicles. That was an expensive policy.

Premiums go up as the coverage gets better and agents who either don't know the difference or just want to bring in a lower price to make a sale may promote the legal liability coverage. I have run across garages that were insured that way, and early on I encountered one who had a burglary with damage to a vehicle. Since the building was locked and the keys were locked, the garage owner was deemed to have taken all necessary precautions and was not liable, and the vehicle was not paid for. Imagine if the entire building burned and all the vehicles being worked on were destroyed. If the fire was not the fault of the garage keeper, there would be no payout.

Let's not forget that some repair and body shops also buy and sell vehicles. In that case, Dealers coverage needs to be placed.

When an agent goes to see a prospective garage client, he should bring a comprehensive checklist to make sure he or she does not miss anything important. Just as importantly, it is incumbent on the agent to educate the prospect on the different coverages and potential losses. You may not get the business, but you must do your due diligence.

Chapter Nineteen: Liability for Contractors

Do you, Mr. Contractor, have enough coverage to protect yourself for the time that you suffer a claim? We know that you do exceptional work, so you will never suffer a claim, right? Wrong!! Statistically wrong. Someone will not like your work, or for some other reason feel compelled to get their money back on work that you did. Or you will be dragged into a lawsuit for which another contractor had responsibility, but the lawyers are looking for deep pockets. You will be named among John Does 1-200.

Example; I had a plumbing contractor get dragged into a lawsuit that involved faulty window installation that was the source of water damage. The plumber did not do any window work.

Or when a general contractor absconded with the money paid him without ordering the work done by his subcontractors. Oh, you are the general? Congratulations; your sub did a poor job and you are getting sued. You don't have to be guilty; just accused. Now you have to defend yourself in court.

So, what do you need?

General Liability, or GL covers you for any damage you do to person or property while you are on the premise. Did you drop a hammer from the second story onto someone walking by, or did you perhaps drop a hammer from a second story onto a car window below?

Products and completed operations: This is part of your Comprehensive General Liability coverage, and covers you for your work after you leave the job: did you leave a nail sticking out that hurt someone later on? Or did your assistant not double check that solder joint and your plumbing job sprang a leak and damaged 10,000 square feet of new wood floor? Oh, by the way, I am not making these examples up. They are all actual claims.

Additional Insured endorsements to your general liability coverage: These add your client onto your policy as an "additional insured." That way, if you are working on his project and create a liability, your insurance is solely responsible. He doesn't have to have his insurance cover the loss or get into a legal battle about responsibility.

If you specialize in commercial work, you will need a products and completed operations endorsement. This will cover your endorsee for the full 10-year statute of limitations on a lawsuit. Your commercial customer and general contractor will demand this type of specific endorsement. Unfortunately, it is not available for residential work, but if you do both, you will need endorsements for both types.

Primary wording endorsement; This assures your endorsee that YOUR insurance policy will be the first to pay for any claims, and they don't have to have their insurance pay it and come after yours for payment (subrogation.)

Oh, and speaking of subrogation, a Waiver of subrogation assures them that you can't come back against them, even if it is their fault. YOUR insurance will pay it, no matter whose fault it is. What a great deal—believe me, they want it and they will demand it

And here is a new wrinkle that you may already have run across: they didn't demand all of the above when you started the job, but now that you want to get paid. All of a sudden a page of requirements shows up as prerequisite to your getting a check. You already did the work and they didn't warn you? Not their problem. Get it, or don't get paid.

New condominium work--an entirely new type of headache:

Let's talk about work on New condominiums. A developer wants to build new condos, which he does. Then he establishes a separate organization called a homeowner's association, to which he transfers all ownership responsibilities after the project is completed. Bad work? Almost always. He can almost always count on being sued for roof work or some other item, because the homeowner's association does not want to exceed the statute of limitations window. For that reason, it is incredibly expensive for an insurance company to insure you if you do new condo work, so most will exclude that from normal policies.

Independent Contractors? NOT. We discussed this in the workers comp section. If you have employees, an employee, someone who might be an employee who works one hour per week, or even someone who gets paid on a 1099, almost certainly, you will need Workers Compensation insurance. The laws changed recently so that the definition of an "independent contractor' has been so narrowed as to become almost nonexistent. The potential penalty for not doing it correctly is $1000 per day per employee who was not insured.

Workers Compensation Waiver of Subrogation: Same thing as for general liability coverage, but the insurance company can charge you by the job, by the year or decline to provide it at all.

Commercial vehicle coverage. This was covered in a prior section as well, but briefly, the coverage is higher; you can get $1,000,000 of coverage, which for a business is not a whole lot. You can also cover it under your commercial umbrella—see below.

And lastly, it can provide Non-owned auto liability coverage. send your assistant to pick up a part in their own car and the get into an accident? Some businesses have workers who use their own vehicles and tools on a job. If they get into an accident while doing work for your business, you could get sued as the employer. If he has insufficient liability limits on his own insurance, you make up the difference, or even all of it if he does not have commercial insurance. Have an installer technician who uses his own vehicle? Good example. You can't be without non-owned auto coverage.

Property Coverage:

Have tools and equipment? Office property? Building? If you work from your home, business property and tools will NOT be covered by your homeowner's insurance. How do I know this? Yep. Been there.

Umbrella

And did I mention that $1,000,000 is not a lot of insurance for a business? If you are getting sued, it will likely be for more than that. If you are doing commercial business, they may want $5,000,000 of coverage before you can get a job. If you do municipal work or sell a product to a very large retailer, you may need $10,000,000 of liability coverage. Excess liability coverage will increase your underlying coverage.

And then there are the contractor and performance bonds. Your client may want a performance or completion bond in order to protect himself from work not being completed. It's very common for large commercial projects, or even smaller ones if the client is a municipality or large company.

Chapter Twenty: Liability for Sales Reps

Insurance that is relevant to sales reps is general liability insurance. If you travel to meet with clients or prospects, you are at risk. Here are the whens and wherefores.

General liability insurance, or commercial general liability (CGL), addresses business claims of bodily injury, medical costs, property damage. You don't have to be guilty, only accused. It can happen when you attend a meeting, meet clients at your office, or even go out to lunch with them

It could happen if a client slips or falls on his OR your premises, or even trips on something you left in the pathway.

If you are at a client's location and you drop something on a piece of equipment or their computer.......oops, property damage has occurred. You are liable.

Completed operations; less likely for sales reps, but if you left something behind that caused injury AFTER YOU ARE GONE FROM THE LOCATION.......oops again--completed ops.

Advertising injury; did you inadvertently slander or infringe on a copyright.

Personal Injury; you feel comfortable enough with the client that you say something libelous against somebody and it backfires on you. That's personal injury; and by the way, it is different from the attorney's definition of personal injury, which is the insurance industry's "bodily injury." Insurance personal injury includes libel, slander, false arrest, wrongful eviction, and discrimination. Remember, you only have to be accused to defend yourself, and that costs money.

Chapter Twenty-One: Restaurant Insurance

Let's say you are a restaurateur and you are having a really bad week; first your chef cut himself while preparing, then your refrigerator died and all your cold-stored food spoiled. Then to top it off, one of your delivery kids got into an accident while making a delivery, and the insurance company is coming after you. Restaurants must be covered for all of those possibilities.

The chef; workers comp coverage

The fridge; equipment breakdown insurance

The food; spoilage coverage

The driver; non-owned auto coverage.

And there is plenty more. Which types of restaurant are you? There are specific types of coverage for each type of food service:

Do you provide table service, and if so, are you a fine dining restaurant, or casual only? Are you fast food? Are you a buffet, cafeteria, smorgasbord, or some of each? If you offer takeout, do you deliver as well? If you are a bar or nightclub, that is a different category with its own set of risks and specific coverage. Country club, mall/shopping center or sandwich bar. It makes a difference as to your insurance coverage, and your workers compensation class code can be affected as well.

Depending on what features your restaurant offers, coverages can vary greatly. Full bar, or wine and beer only? Do you have entertainment, a dance floor? Do you cater? Are you renting out space for events, banquets or private parties? If you have off-site events or are you a promoter? That is yet another type of coverage. Do you have parking, and if so, do you have valet? Yours, or a subcontractor's? Are they covering you in case they hurt someone or something while on your property? How is your ANSUL system? Does it cover your deep fryer? Your fish tank could leak and cause damage, or even do damage to a customer? Do you have coat check, storage of entertainers' equipment or other property of others? Are you compliant with ADA, or are you vulnerable to lawsuit?

Here are some other coverages you may require: premises liability, product liability in case your food poisons someone or they claim it did, property coverage for your fixtures, building coverage if you own the building or are on a triple-net lease, advertising, and leased property.

This is another situation where a checklist is critical for an agent to use. There are too many opportunities to leave something out.

Chapter Twenty-Two: Homeowners Associations

HOA coverage also can be pretty complicated, and there are there are a number of conditions which may cause an increase in premiums. Let's take a closer look at the background and the elements involved in coverage and in producing rates.

An HOA is a private association, formed with the purpose of managing a residential subdivision. Their exact responsibilities and powers are dictated by a governing document called the CC&Rs, or Contracts, Covenants and Restrictions. A subsection called Bylaws are the exact rules by which the association operates, including creating a managing board of directors, elections, responsibilities, job descriptions, levying fines and more. Together these are the governing documents.

The above documents also define the exact responsibilities of the association vs the members in matters such as how much and what type of insurance must be obtained by the HOA.

Each year, various sections of California laws are updated with respect to what HOAs are allowed to do and what they are required to do, as well as how they are restricted. The first development tract in which I was an owner, for example, disallowed the sale of the homes to Jews. Moving into that complex, and having purchased my home from a Jewish family, I was unaware of those sections of the CC&Rs, and clearly, by the time the first family had purchased their home, the Civil Rights laws had preempted that CC&R clause.

In recent years, a number of discrimination cases were filed and settled, causing payments to be made by HOAs. This threat of increased risk can drive up rates for all HOAs as insurance carriers prepare for possible battles in the courts.

So, what types of HOAs exist?

There are some associations, which only manage the common areas of single-family homes in a community. Those are called planned unit developments, or PUDs. They make sure that there is visual uniformity in appearance of the homes and that the grounds are kept.

There are some associations which are responsible for the actual structure of the buildings. This is especially true in the case of condominiums and townhomes but can apply to single family units and duplex units within the community as well. All of these powers and responsibilities are defined by the governing documents.

An HOA may be responsible for insuring interior floors, cabinets and other structures within each unit? These responsibilities are defined by the governing documents as well, and these responsibilities vary from HOA to HOA.

So, what are the relevant parts of the insurance policy for an HOA? Remember that individual unit owners must procure supplemental coverage that protects the portions of their unit that are not protected by the master HOA insurance.

Property first. What coverage is needed in order to properly insure property to value? Should coverage be just for exterior walls, or should it include those kitchen cabinets and floors? How about other fixtures, walls, tile and so on? And what value should be placed on all of the property that will allow proper replacement after a loss?

The cost of materials has a lot to do with property coverage rates. As building materials become more expensive, property pricing goes up. Insurance companies sometimes have automatic increases, which may or may not be necessary—it's an area for review.

And how about common area equipment and structures, such as pool equipment, recreation equipment, fences, pools, spas and dozens of other items owned in common by the members of the association. All of these must go into the consideration of total insured value.

Then what is a reasonable deductible to apply to coverage? Do you want it to apply to the smallest loss, or are you a risk taker as an association and want a higher deductible? How much higher? This must be explored and matched with the requirements of the governing documents, which may dictate the amounts of coverage.

Is the coverage for replacement cost at full value, or depreciated value like a car? A loss could hurt—badly by the time you depreciate value and subtract your deductible. Availability of the most comprehensive coverage may be dictated by prior losses and current maintenance, or lack thereof.

What other areas should be considered?

Liability coverage: Will it cover just physical damage that a member might do against a non-owner or some other third party, or their property? How broad, exactly is the liability coverage included in the policy?

Is the liability coverage limit only $1,000,000? Really? 200 units in the group, $40,000,000 of assets, and you think a lawsuit is going to stop at $1,000,000? Let's plan for a worse-case scenario, or even the worst-case scenario, with more coverage. Excess liability insurance is now needed.

I know of one claim levied by a renter in a complex against the handyman of the complex, claiming he touched her inappropriately. Will the master policy's liability insurance cover that, or will the association be writing a big check? Not guilty? Prove it. and by the time you prove it, how much have you spent in legal fees? Pay to make it go away? How much will that take?

And speaking of handymen, does the HOA have employees? If so, it will certainly need workers compensation coverage, because as an employer, the law requires that employee workers are protected from injury.

Do the employees drive their own vehicle for the HOA to pick up supplies? Do the board members run errands in their own vehicles? Do they run for stamps, food for a party? There is a coverage for that as well, in case they are involved in an accident while doing work for the HOA. There is that non-owned auto coverage again that was mentioned in the commercial vehicle chapter of this book.

And speaking of board members, they are directors and officers of your HOA. There is a possible scenario in which the HOA members hold them responsible for errors in judgment, or even just perceived errors in judgment or management. Is the board covered for that? If you are a board member, did you sign on to work part time for nothing and be vulnerable to a lawsuit for doing what you thought was best? The proper coverage for such protection is called Directors and Officers coverage.

Oh, and by the way, the Treasurer is bound to be in charge of plenty of money. Is the HOA covered in the event that he or she decides to use HOA monies to fund a trip to the Caribbean.......permanently?

Does the HOA operate a website? It could be accused of infecting any visitors. There is cyber liability coverage available with most insurance packages.

Is someone keeping track of buying and maintaining internet certificates for the website? Website security updates? Even if not infecting, if the HOA is accused of it and sued, it must still mount a legal defense. That can cost.

And finally, let's talk about my favorite; earthquake coverage. Is it in place? Great; how is it structured? What is the deductible? What assets are covered? Is it simple building coverage, for earthquake, or does it cover more, like your foundations, pollution, mold, debris removal? There is plenty to consider.

Acknowledgments

I would be remiss if I didn't thank my wife of more than thirty years for her support. This has not been a journey without road bumps. Thank you Gloria for joining me on the road.

About the Author

Well, first it would be helpful to know a bit about the author. He started innocently enough, at two or three years old. Disassembled a clock and then an electric iron just to see how they worked and of course, couldn't reassemble them

He is a tinkerer and a technical person.

Marc taught himself enough music so that after one year of playing guitar, he could have a student, then two, then 300 and work my way through college. He learned enough photography to be able to shoot two weddings, enough videography to shoot short films, then eight YouTube videos. he somehow ended up with a graduate degree in a biochemistry field instead of engineering, which would have been more suitable, BUT learned enough nuclear chemistry to teach a workshop to the department that he headed at a large medical laboratory; learned enough aeronautics to scratch build flying models and the machines to cut complex foam wings. There have been a number of other technical fields he has have dabbled in; electronic design, simple programming, computers, leather working arts and so on. You will get the idea. He likes the technical stuff.

Marc's first impression of insurance was from a Woody Allen film, where as an insurance agent he harassed what he thought was a prospect into an elevator and out again on a different floor, keeping up an obnoxious and continuous stream of sales pitch. He certainly didn't want to be that guy. But circumstances dictated he go into insurance and now is in his thirty sixth year as a full-time insurance agent. Hopefully not obnoxious.

One thing to know for sure is that insurance is a technical field. Sure, there is the selling, but to understand what you are selling, you have to be technical. If you don't understand it, you may omit an important coverage, and then, at the worst time, you get a phone call at one o'clock in the morning advising you that someone's home or business has had a loss. Then you rush to the office to make sure you provided the right and complete coverage for your client.

The other thing is that you have to like people or it won't work. You must want to help others. That's the real job. New clients know that and along the way, if you are lucky, they get to see that.

So, the technical lead to the business. Marc actually did not choose it. it chose Marc through a series of professional stumbles in a working career.

Thanks to all of you who have bought this book.

If you like this book, please give it a good review. If you have personal comments and would like to contact Marc, just email marc@schwartzwork.com, or leave a comment on the website at www.thecsia.com.

www.ingramcontent.com/pod-product-compliance
Lightning Source LLC
Chambersburg PA
CBHW071045220526
45467CB00004B/1687